365 Daily Pearls of Wisdom

quotes for
inspired living

Sarah,

Happy 13th Birthday

April 10, 2020

Love you!

Grandpa & Grandma

DEDICATION

I dedicate this book to my children,
Aidan & Kyra.

Thank you for choosing me to be your
mother. It's my greatest honor. I love you
with every piece of my heart.

Before 2010, I would never have dreamed of compiling a day book of inspirational quotes to share with others. I wasn't terribly inspired. I was living life asleep at the wheel.

The universe has a funny way of delivering lessons to wake us from our slumbers. Mine came in two forms. First, my amazing father was diagnosed with stage IV lung cancer. Second, just 9 days before he passed away from cancer, I was diagnosed with a slow-growing brain cancer. I had 2 young children and a husband. I didn't want my children to live without a mother. I hated the thought of that. My life was turned upside down.

I could have sunk into self-pity. I could have played the victim card, but somewhere deep inside of me, I could feel a spring of power beginning to surge. I felt like there was a reason for my predicament, that there was something I was meant to learn and share through this experience. I didn't want my life to be over, especially since I had always *waited* to start living. I had a lot of conditions around my happiness. I was the person that always thought "I'll be happy when...", "I'll do this when...".

I began a journey of awesome self-discovery all thanks to the health issue that scares most people more than any other. I found the opportunity in the challenge. It was as if God was saying to me "Erin, I tried to get you to pay attention to your feelings and what you truly wanted, but you were too stubborn and afraid to change so I am giving you this gift. If you see it as a gift, you will be blessed in more ways than you can realize, but if you fear it and let it take your power away further, you will see it as a curse." The universe took it up a notch in June 2016 when I faced intense head pain and found myself back at the hospital for a craniotomy. With all my knowledge that I had learned in the previous 6 years, I was still fearful and went through a crisis of confidence and a bout with lazy living where I just wanted to be like everybody else and therefore ate much more processed crap than was good for me. Before the surgery I was mentally checked out and craving junk food. I awoke from the surgery, however, transformed. I needed the crisis to awaken my inner power. For six years I had intellectually known what to do, but when nothing feels wrong (no pain or dysfunction) it can be hard to motivate to do what you know is best for you. I awoke finely tuned to only want to eat food full of vitality, I awoke able to feel the chaotic energy of emf radiation from cell phones, and I awoke knowing that my 'diagnosis' was a vehicle of rapid spiritual understanding, showing me that I have a power within me to use this beautiful, dynamic energy (not something to loathe and fear) to transform me like a caterpillar becomes a butterfly. I found blessings in this challenge and it brought me roaring back to messy, lesson-filled and glorious life.

The challenges we face are powerful catalysts for change

IF we embrace them rather than fear them. Positive thinking has the power to reframe your challenges, allowing you to see opportunities for growth and change. I am a better mother, wife, friend and human being as a result of my challenge. I would never want to go back to the pre-brain tumor version of myself. Ever.

I chose the title *365 Daily Pearls of Wisdom* because I equate a brain tumor to a pearl. The pearl is known as the queen of gems and is the only gem made from a living organism. It is created when an irritant, like a grain of sand, gets past the oyster's protective mantle. The oyster begins to coat the foreign substance with nacre, mother of pearl, to protect itself. I have read some scientists argue that tumors, our own immune system's response to irritation, are very much the same. They protect the body the same way a pearl protects the oyster. Over time, this substance which causes the oyster stress transforms into one of the most treasured substances on earth. I have found on my journey that the brain tumor is exactly the same. It protects me at the deepest level because it encourages me to follow my soul's guidance. It also gave me a voice and a mission. If I kept living the way I did before the diagnosis, both mentally and physically, I'd be dead. The brain tumor called me to change and I heeded the call.

Do you know someone who has been through a cancer journey? Often these people transform the way they live. They do things they always put off. They pursue their deep callings and worry far less about conforming and playing it safe. They have had a taste of the fleetingness of life and don't want to waste another minute. The brain tumor inspired me to start living authentically and as true to my soul callings as I could muster. Sometimes that's hard because the soul and the ego are not always on the same page, but when I am truest to my feelings, my health reflects it.

I used to wake up and immediately think of the laundry list of 'to dos' and daily stresses that I had waiting for me. What a waste! I compiled this collection of inspirational quotes to give you a tool to start each day connected to empowerment, peace and purpose. Keep this book next to your bed, read the daily message and set yourself on the right path every morning. Our attitude dictates how we feel. When you change your pattern of thinking your life has no choice but to reflect that too.

To your well-being,

Erin

JANUARY 1

Start by doing what's necessary; then do what's possible; and suddenly you are doing the impossible.

St. Francis of Assisi

JANUARY 2

You are under no obligation to be the same person you were five minutes ago.

Unknown

JANUARY 3

There are only two ways to live your life. One is as though nothing is a miracle. The other is as though everything is a miracle.

Albert Einstein

JANUARY 4

Security is mostly a superstition. It does not exist in nature, nor do the children of men as a whole experience it. Avoiding danger is no safer in the long run than outright exposure. Life is either a daring adventure, or nothing.

Helen Keller

JANUARY 5

I can't change the direction of the
wind, but I can adjust my sails to
always reach my destination.

Jimmy Dean

JANUARY 6

Try to be a rainbow in someone's cloud.

Maya Angelou

JANUARY 7

The things that we love tell us what we are.

Thomas Aquinas

JANUARY 8

Nothing is impossible, the word itself
says 'I'm possible!

Audrey Hepburn

JANUARY 9

Change your thoughts and you change your world.

Norman Vincent Peale

JANUARY 10

If opportunity doesn't knock, build a door.

Milton Berle

JANUARY 11

Believe you can and you're halfway there.

Theodore Roosevelt

JANUARY 12

Inaction breeds doubt and fear. Action breeds confidence and courage. If you want to conquer fear, do not sit home and think about it. Go out and get busy.

Dale Carnegie

JANUARY 13

The measure of who we are is what we
do with what we have.

Vince Lombardi

JANUARY 14

Your task is not to seek for love, but
merely to seek and find all the barriers
within yourself that you have built
against it.

Rumi

JANUARY 15

Follow your bliss and the universe will open doors where there were only walls.

Joseph Campbell

JANUARY 16

Today I choose life. Every morning
when I wake up I can choose joy,
happiness, negativity, pain... To feel the
freedom that comes from being able to
continue to make mistakes and choices -
today I choose to feel life, not to deny
my humanity but embrace it.

Kevyn Aucoin

JANUARY 17

Two roads diverged in a wood and I - I took the one less traveled by, and that has made all the difference.

Robert Frost

JANUARY 18

A life spent making mistakes is not only more honorable, but more useful than a life spent doing nothing.

George Bernard Shaw

JANUARY 19

There are two ways of spreading light:
to be the candle or the mirror that
reflects it.

Edith Wharton

JANUARY 20

Your big opportunity may be right
where you are now.

Napoleon Hill

JANUARY 21

Thousands of candles can be lighted from a single candle, and the life of the candle will not be shortened. Happiness never decreases by being shared.

Buddha

JANUARY 22

If you always put limits on everything you do, physical or anything else, it will spread into your work and into your life. There are no limits. There are only plateaus, and you must not stay there, you must go beyond them.

Bruce Lee

JANUARY 23

People tell you the world looks a certain way. Parents tell you how to think. Schools tell you how to think. TV. Religion. And then at a certain point, if you're lucky, you realize you can make up your own mind. Nobody sets the rules but you. You can design your own life.

Carrie-Anne Moss

JANUARY 24

Life is a succession of lessons which
must be lived to be understood.

Helen Keller

JANUARY 25

Out of difficulties grow miracles.

Jean de la Bruyere

JANUARY 26

Don't judge each day by the harvest you reap but by the seeds that you plant.

Robert Louis Stevenson

JANUARY 27

The world is full of magical things patiently waiting for our wits to grow sharper.

Bertrand Russell

JANUARY 28

You will never be happy if you continue
to search for what happiness consists of.
You will never live if you are looking for
the meaning of life.

Albert Camus

JANUARY 29

What lies behind you and what lies in front of you, pales in comparison to what lies inside of you.

Ralph Waldo Emerson

JANUARY 30

We must let go of the life we have planned, so as to accept the one that is waiting for us.

Joseph Campbell

JANUARY 31

If you accept the expectations of others, especially negative ones, then you never will change the outcome.

Michael Jordan

FEBRUARY 1

To the mind that is still, the whole
universe surrenders.

Lao Tzu

FEBRUARY 2

You must do the things you think you
cannot do.

Eleanor Roosevelt

FEBRUARY 3

Try to be like the turtle - at ease in your own shell.

Bill Copeland

FEBRUARY 4

When we seek to discover the best in others, we somehow bring out the best in ourselves.

William Arthur Ward

FEBRUARY 5

If we did all the things we are capable of, we would literally astound ourselves.

Thomas A. Edison

FEBRUARY 6

What we need is more people who
specialize in the impossible.

Theodore Roethke

FEBRUARY 7

Cherish your visions and your dreams
as they are the children of your soul, the
blueprints of your ultimate
achievements.

Napoleon Hill

FEBRUARY 8

Man never made any material as resilient as the human spirit.

Bernard Williams

FEBRUARY 9

Your present circumstances don't determine where you can go; they merely determine where you start.

Nido Qubein

FEBRUARY 10

The best way out is always through.

Robert Frost

FEBRUARY 11

Only those who will risk going too far can possibly find out how far one can go.

T. S. Eliot

FEBRUARY 12

Clouds come floating into my life, no longer to carry rain or usher storm, but to add color to my sunset sky.

Rabindranath Tagore

FEBRUARY 13

That it will never come again is what
makes life sweet.

Emily Dickinson

FEBRUARY 14

Let us always meet each other with
smile, for the smile is the beginning of
love.

Mother Teresa

FEBRUARY 15

If a man does not keep pace with his companions, perhaps it is because he hears a different drummer. Let him step to the music which he hears, however measured or far away.

Henry David Thoreau

FEBRUARY 16

Attitude is a little thing that makes a
big difference.

Winston Churchill

FEBRUARY 17

I have always believed, and I still
believe, that whatever good or bad
fortune may come our way we can
always give it meaning and transform it
into something of value.

Hermann Hesse

FEBRUARY 18

Whatever you vividly imagine, ardently desire, sincerely believe, and enthusiastically act upon... must inevitably come to pass!

Paul J. Meyer

FEBRUARY 19

One of the greatest paradoxes of your physical senses is that your eyes actually show you what you believe, not what you see.

Mike Dooley

FEBRUARY 20

The most authentic thing about us is our capacity to create, to overcome, to endure, to transform, to love and to be greater than our suffering.

Ben Okri

FEBRUARY 21

Find out who you are and be that person. That's what your soul was put on this Earth to be. Find that truth, live that truth and everything else will come.

Ellen DeGeneres

FEBRUARY 22

From what we get, we can make a living; what we give, however, makes a life.

Arthur Ashe

FEBRUARY 23

Learning how to be still, to really be still
and let life happen - that stillness
becomes a radiance.

Morgan Freeman

FEBRUARY 24

Act like you expect to get into the end zone.

Christopher Morley

FEBRUARY 25

The purpose of life is a life of purpose.

Robert Byrne

FEBRUARY 26

We can change our lives. We can do, have, and be exactly what we wish.

Tony Robbins

FEBRUARY 27

Nurture your minds with great thoughts. To believe in the heroic makes heroes.

Benjamin Disraeli

FEBRUARY 28

There is just one life for each of us:
our own.

Euripides

FEBRUARY 29

The Wright brothers flew right through
the smoke screen of impossibility.

Charles Kettering

MARCH 1

I believe there's an inner power that makes winners or losers. And the winners are the ones who really listen to the truth of their hearts.

Sylvester Stallone

MARCH 2

Most of us have far more courage than we ever dreamed we possessed.

Dale Carnegie

MARCH 3

I've been absolutely terrified every moment of my life - and I've never let it keep me from doing a single thing I wanted to do.

Georgia O'Keeffe

MARCH 4

The greatest discovery of any generation
is that a human being can alter his life
by altering his attitude.

William James

MARCH 5

My mission in life is not merely to survive, but to thrive; and to do so with some passion, some compassion, some humor, and some style.

Maya Angelou

MARCH 6

Do your little bit of good where you are;
it's those little bits of good put together
that overwhelm the world.

Desmond Tutu

MARCH 7

True change takes place in the
imagination.

Unknown

MARCH 8

Each day provides its own gifts.

Marcus Aurelius

MARCH 9

I believe that one defines oneself by reinvention. To not be like your parents. To not be like your friends. To be yourself. To cut yourself out of stone.

Henry Rollins

MARCH 10

There is a loftier ambition than merely to stand high in the world. It is to stoop down and lift mankind a little higher.

Henry Van Dyke

MARCH 11

I said to the almond tree, 'Friend, speak to me of God,' and the almond tree blossomed.

Nikos Kazantzakis

MARCH 12

Let each man exercise the art
he knows.

Aristophanes

MARCH 13

I celebrate myself, and sing myself.

Walt Whitman

MARCH 14

Our time here is magic! It's the only
space you have to realize whatever it is
that is beautiful, whatever is true,
whatever is great, whatever is potential,
whatever is rare, whatever is unique, in.
It's the only space.

Ben Okri

MARCH 15

Belief creates the actual fact.

William James

MARCH 16

Think with your whole body.

Taisen Deshimaru

MARCH 17

The authentic self is the soul made
visible.

Sarah Ban Breathnach

MARCH 18

Failure will never overtake me if my determination to succeed is strong enough.

Og Mandino

MARCH 19

Your talent is God's gift to you. What you do with it is your gift back to God.

Leo Buscaglia

MARCH 20

A creative man is motivated by the desire to achieve, not by the desire to beat others.

Ayn Rand

MARCH 21

It does not matter how slowly you go
as long as you do not stop.

Confucius

MARCH 22

Infuse your life with action. Don't wait for it to happen. Make it happen. Make your own future. Make your own hope. Make your own love. And whatever your beliefs, honor your creator, not by passively waiting for grace to come down from upon high, but by doing what you can to make grace happen... yourself, right now, right down here on Earth.

Bradley Whitford

MARCH 23

Believe in yourself! Have faith in your abilities! Without a humble but reasonable confidence in your own powers you cannot be successful or happy.

Norman Vincent Peale

MARCH 24

Our greatest weakness lies in giving up.
The most certain way to succeed is
always to try just one more time.

Thomas A. Edison

MARCH 25

The secret of getting ahead is
getting started.

Mark Twain

MARCH 26

If you can dream it, you can do it.

Walt Disney

MARCH 27

Our attitudes control our lives.
Attitudes are a secret power working
twenty-four hours a day, for good or
bad. It is of paramount importance that
we know how to harness and control
this great force.

Irving Berlin

MARCH 28

The most courageous act is still to think
for yourself. Aloud.

Coco Chanel

MARCH 29

Expect problems and eat them for
breakfast.

Alfred A. Montapert

MARCH 30

Start where you are. Use what you
have. Do what you can.

Arthur Ashe

MARCH 31

In order to succeed, we must first
believe that we can.

Nikos Kazantzakis

APRIL 1

Optimism is the faith that leads to achievement. Nothing can be done without hope and confidence.

Helen Keller

APRIL 2

I know where I'm going and I know the truth, and I don't have to be what you want me to be. I'm free to be what I want.

Muhammad Ali

APRIL 3

What you get by achieving your goals is not as important as what you become by achieving your goals.

Zig Ziglar

APRIL 4

Darkness cannot drive out darkness;
only light can do that. Hate cannot drive
out hate; only love can do that.

Martin Luther King, Jr.

APRIL 5

Perseverance is failing 19 times and succeeding the 20th.

Julie Andrews

APRIL 6

You are not here merely to make a living. You are here in order to enable the world to live more amply, with greater vision, with a finer spirit of hope and achievement. You are here to enrich the world, and you impoverish yourself if you forget the errand.

Woodrow Wilson

APRIL 7

If you're going through hell,
keep going.

Winston Churchill

APRIL 8

I attribute my success to this - I never gave or took any excuse.

Florence Nightingale

APRIL 9

There is no passion to be found playing small - in settling for a life that is less than the one you are capable of living.

Nelson Mandela

<u>APRIL 10</u>

If you don't like something, change it. If you can't change it, change your attitude.

Maya Angelou

APRIL 11

Either I will find a way, or I will make one.

Philip Sidney

<u>APRIL 12</u>

If you don't design your own life plan, chances are you'll fall into someone else's plan. And guess what they have planned for you? Not much.

Jim Rohn

APRIL 13

Life's too short to wake up with regrets. So love the people who treat you right, forgive the ones who don't and believe that everything happens for a reason. If you get a chance, take it. If it changes your life, let it. Nobody said it'd be easy, they just promised it would be worth it.

Dr. Seuss

APRIL 14

If you want to succeed you should strike out on new paths, rather than travel the worn paths of accepted success.

John D. Rockefeller

APRIL 15

Do the one thing you think you cannot do. Fail at it. Try again. Do better the second time. The only people who never tumble are those who never mount the high wire. This is your moment. Own it.

Oprah Winfrey

APRIL 16

When something is important enough,
you do it even if the odds are not in
your favor.

Elon Musk

APRIL 17

Life is a tide; float on it. Go down with it and go up with it, but be detached. Then it is not difficult.

Prem Rawat

APRIL 18

So often times it happens that we live our lives in chains and we never even know we have the key.

The Eagles

APRIL 19

Set your sights high, the higher the better. Expect the most wonderful things to happen, not in the future but right now. Realize that nothing is too good. Allow absolutely nothing to hamper you or hold you up in any way.

Eileen Caddy

APRIL 20

Do or do not.
There is no try.

Yoda

APRIL 21

There are powers inside of you which, if you could discover and use, would make of you everything you ever dreamed or imagined you could become.

Orison Swett Marden

APRIL 22

When I run after what I think I want,
my days are a furnace of stress and
anxiety; if I sit in my own place of
patience, what I need flows to me, and
without pain. From this I understand
that what I want also wants me, is
looking for me and attracting me. There
is a great secret here for anyone who can
grasp it.

Rumi

APRIL 23

You just can't beat the person who
never gives up.

Babe Ruth

APRIL 24

Do not wait; the time will never be 'just right.' Start where you stand, and work with whatever tools you may have at your command, and better tools will be found as you go along.

George Herbert

APRIL 25

I'd rather attempt to do something great
and fail than to attempt to do nothing
and succeed.

Robert H. Schuller

APRIL 26

If you change the way you look at things, the things you look at change.

Wayne Dyer

APRIL 27

You simply have to put one foot in front of the other and keep going. Put blinders on and plow right ahead.

George Lucas

APRIL 28

Natural forces within us are the true
healers of disease.

Hippocrates

APRIL 29

Dream as if you'll live forever. Live as if you'll die today.

James Dean

APRIL 30

The first step toward success is taken when you refuse to be a captive of the environment in which you first find yourself.

Mark Caine

MAY 1

Perseverance is not a long race; it is many short races one after the other.

Walter Elliot

<u>MAY 2</u>

The more man meditates upon good thoughts, the better will be his world and the world at large.

Confucius

MAY 3

Big shots are only little shots who keep shooting.

Christopher Morley

MAY 4

We are taught you must blame your father, your sisters, your brothers, the school, the teachers - but never blame yourself. It's never your fault. But it's always your fault, because if you wanted to change you're the one who has got to change.

Katharine Hepburn

<u>MAY 5</u>

Nothing ever goes away until it teaches us what we need to know.

Pema Chodron

<u>MAY 6</u>

Dreams are necessary to life.

Anais Nin

MAY 7

All life is an experiment. The more experiments you make the better.

Ralph Waldo Emerson

MAY 8

Only when we are no longer afraid
do we begin to live.

Dorothy Thompson

MAY 9

Every exit is an entry somewhere else.

Tom Stoppard

MAY 10

I am not afraid... I was born to do this.

Joan of Arc

MAY 11

If you ask me what I came into this life to do, I will tell you: I came to live out loud.

Emile Zola

MAY 12

Always continue the climb. It is possible for you to do whatever you choose, if you first get to know who you are and are willing to work with a power that is greater than ourselves to do it.

Ella Wheeler Wilcox

<u>MAY 13</u>

Leap, and the net will appear.

John Burroughs

<u>MAY 14</u>

Be miserable. Or motivate yourself.
Whatever has to be done, it's always
your choice.

Wayne Dyer

<u>MAY 15</u>

Did I offer peace today? Did I bring a smile to someone's face? Did I say words of healing? Did I let go of my anger and resentment? Did I forgive? Did I love? These are the real questions. I must trust that the little bit of love that I sow now will bear many fruits, here in this world and the life to come.

Henri Nouwen

<u>MAY 16</u>

You're going to go through tough times
- that's life. But I say, 'Nothing happens
to you, it happens for you.' See the
positive in negative events.

Joel Osteen

MAY 17

The key is to keep company only with people who uplift you, whose presence calls forth your best.

Epictetus

MAY 18

Your attitude is like a box of crayons that color your world. Constantly color your picture gray, and your picture will always be bleak. Try adding some bright colors to the picture by including humor, and your picture begins to lighten up.

Allen Klein

<u>MAY 19</u>

Life must be lived as play.

Plato

MAY 20

Positive thinking will let you do everything better than negative thinking will.

Zig Ziglar

MAY 21

You've done it before and you can do it now. See the positive possibilities. Redirect the substantial energy of your frustration and turn it into positive, effective, unstoppable determination.

Ralph Marston

<u>MAY 22</u>

My dear friend, clear your mind of can't.

Samuel Johnson

MAY 23

Here is the world. Beautiful and terrible
things will happen. Don't be afraid.

Frederick Buechner

MAY 24

Very little is needed to make a happy life; it is all within yourself, in your way of thinking.

Marcus Aurelius

MAY 25

Throughout life people will make you mad, disrespect you and treat you bad. Let God deal with the things they do, cause hate in your heart will consume you too.

Will Smith

<u>MAY 26</u>

In the end, it's not the years in your life
that count. It's the life in your years.

Abraham Lincoln

<u>MAY 27</u>

One way to get the most out of life is to look upon it as an adventure.

William Feather

MAY 28

The true secret of happiness lies in taking a genuine interest in all the details of daily life.

William Morris

MAY 29

Some people say I have attitude - maybe I do... but I think you have to. You have to believe in yourself when no one else does - that makes you a winner right there.

Venus Williams

<u>MAY 30</u>

Life is a series of natural and spontaneous changes. Don't resist them - that only creates sorrow. Let reality be reality. Let things flow naturally forward in whatever way they like.

Lao Tzu

MAY 31

My life is my message.

Mahatma Gandhi

JUNE 1

Our life always expresses the result of
our dominant thoughts.

Soren Kierkegaard

JUNE 2

We need to give each other the space to grow, to be ourselves, to exercise our diversity. We need to give each other space so that we may both give and receive such beautiful things as ideas, openness, dignity, joy, healing, and inclusion.

Max de Pree

JUNE 3

Life is a mirror and will reflect back to the thinker what he thinks into it.

Ernest Holmes

JUNE 4

Character develops itself in the stream
of life.

Johann Wolfgang von Goethe

JUNE 5

Beware the barrenness of a busy life.

Socrates

JUNE 6

We must be willing to let go of the life
we have planned, so as to have the life
that is waiting for us.

E. M. Forster

JUNE 7

I have a simple philosophy: Fill what's empty. Empty what's full. Scratch where it itches.

Alice Roosevelt Longworth

JUNE 8

The greatest trap in our life is not success, popularity or power, but self-rejection.

Henri Nouwen

JUNE 9

What if you gave someone a gift, and they neglected to thank you for it - would you be likely to give them another? Life is the same way. In order to attract more of the blessings that life has to offer, you must truly appreciate what you already have.

Ralph Marston

JUNE 10

It takes half your life before you discover life is a do-it-yourself project.

Napoleon Hill

JUNE 11

What we play is life.

Louis Armstrong

JUNE 12

It's best to have failure happen early in life. It wakes up the Phoenix bird in you so you rise from the ashes.

Anne Baxter

JUNE 13

The golden moments in the stream of life rush past us, and we see nothing but sand; the angels come to visit us, and we only know them when they are gone.

George Eliot

JUNE 14

Nearly all the best things that came to me in life have been unexpected, unplanned by me.

Carl Sandburg

<u>JUNE 15</u>

Don't let life discourage you; everyone who got where he is had to begin where he was.

Richard L. Evans

JUNE 16

Don't go through life,
grow through life.

Eric Butterworth

JUNE 17

Your work is going to fill a large part of your life, and the only way to be truly satisfied is to do what you believe is great work. And the only way to do great work is to love what you do. If you haven't found it yet, keep looking. Don't settle. As with all matters of the heart, you'll know when you find it.

Steve Jobs

JUNE 18

Your destiny is to fulfill those things upon which you focus most intently. So choose to keep your focus on that which is truly magnificent, beautiful, uplifting and joyful. Your life is always moving toward something.

Ralph Marston

JUNE 19

There are two great days in a person's life - the day we are born and the day we discover why.

William Barclay

JUNE 20

Believe that life is worth living and your belief will help create the fact.

William James

JUNE 21

Bad things do happen; how I respond to them defines my character and the quality of my life. I can choose to sit in perpetual sadness, immobilized by the gravity of my loss, or I can choose to rise from the pain and treasure the most precious gift I have - life itself.

Walter Anderson

JUNE 22

Take up one idea. Make that one idea your life - think of it, dream of it, live on that idea. Let the brain, muscles, nerves, every part of your body, be full of that idea, and just leave every other idea alone. This is the way to success.

Swami Vivekananda

JUNE 23

I've missed more than 9,000 shots in my career. I've lost almost 300 games. 26 times, I've been trusted to take the game winning shot and missed. I've failed over and over and over again in my life. And that is why I succeed.

Michael Jordan

JUNE 24

Life is 10% what happens to me and 90% how I react to it.

Charles Swindoll

JUNE 25

Courage is being scared to death... and saddling up anyway.

John Wayne

JUNE 26

Choose a job you love, and you will never have to work a day in your life.

Confucius

JUNE 27

God gave us the gift of life; it is up to us to give ourselves the gift of living well.

Voltaire

JUNE 28

All you need in this life is ignorance and confidence, and then success is sure.

Mark Twain

JUNE 29

Beginning today, treat everyone you meet as if they were going to be dead by midnight. Extend to them all the care, kindness and understanding you can muster, and do it with no thought of any reward. Your life will never be the same again.

Og Mandino

JUNE 30

Remembering that I'll be dead soon is the most important tool I've ever encountered to help me make the big choices in life. Because almost everything - all external expectations, all pride, all fear of embarrassment or failure - these things just fall away in the face of death, leaving only what is truly important.

Steve Jobs

JULY 1

Life is a series of experiences, each one of which makes us bigger, even though sometimes it is hard to realize this. For the world was built to develop character, and we must learn that the setbacks and grieves which we endure help us in our marching onward.

Henry Ford

JULY 2

There is no passion to be found playing small - in settling for a life that is less than the one you are capable of living.

Nelson Mandela

JULY 3

We make a living by what we get, but
we make a life by what we give.

Winston Churchill

JULY 4

We hold these truths to be self-evident: that all men are created equal; that they are endowed by their Creator with certain unalienable rights; that among these are life, liberty, and the pursuit of happiness.

Thomas Jefferson

<u>JULY 5</u>

All the adversity I've had in my life, all my troubles and obstacles, have strengthened me... You may not realize it when it happens, but a kick in the teeth may be the best thing in the world for you.

Walt Disney

JULY 6

When we meet real tragedy in life, we can react in two ways - either by losing hope and falling into self-destructive habits, or by using the challenge to find our inner strength. Thanks to the teachings of Buddha, I have been able to take this second way.

Dalai Lama

JULY 7

If you wish to succeed in life, make perseverance your bosom friend, experience your wise counselor, caution your elder brother, and hope your guardian genius.

Joseph Addison

JULY 8

Stop acting as if life is a rehearsal. Live this day as if it were your last. The past is over and gone. The future is not guaranteed.

Wayne Dyer

JULY 9

In school, you're taught a lesson and then given a test. In life, you're given a test that teaches you a lesson.

Tom Bodett

JULY 10

When you rise in the morning, give thanks for the light, for your life, for your strength. Give thanks for your food and for the joy of living. If you see no reason to give thanks, the fault lies in yourself.

Tecumseh

JULY 11

The biggest adventure you can take is to live the life of your dreams.

Oprah Winfrey

<u>JULY 12</u>

If one advances confidently in the
direction of his dreams, and endeavors
to live the life which he has imagined,
he will meet with a success unexpected
in common hours.

Henry David Thoreau

JULY 13

There is a fountain of youth: it is your mind, your talents, the creativity you bring to your life and the lives of people you love. When you learn to tap this source, you will truly have defeated age.

Sophia Loren

JULY 14

We are here to add what we can to life, not to get what we can from life.

William Osler

JULY 15

It's not an accident that musicians become musicians and engineers become engineers: it's what they're born to do. If you can tune into your purpose and really align with it, setting goals so that your vision is an expression of that purpose, then life flows much more easily.

Jack Canfield

<u>JULY 16</u>

Take a chance! All life is a chance. The man who goes farthest is generally the one who is willing to do and dare.

Dale Carnegie

JULY 17

Life shrinks or expands in proportion
to one's courage.

Anais Nin

JULY 18

Life is like a ten speed bicycle. Most of us have gears we never use.

Charles M. Schulz

JULY 19

It is possible to become discouraged about the injustice we see everywhere. But God did not promise us that the world would be humane and just. He gives us the gift of life and allows us to choose the way we will use our limited time on earth. It is an awesome opportunity.

Cesar Chavez

<u>JULY 20</u>

It takes courage to grow up and become
who you really are.

E. E. Cummings

JULY 21

Success is not final, failure is not fatal: it is the courage to continue that counts.

Winston Churchill

JULY 22

Life is what we make it, always has been, always will be.

Grandma Moses

JULY 23

Success is nothing more than a few simple disciplines, practiced every day.

Jim Rohn

JULY 24

The starting point of all achievement
is desire.

Napoleon Hill

JULY 25

Your time is limited, so don't waste it living someone else's life. Don't be trapped by dogma - which is living with the results of other people's thinking. Don't let the noise of others' opinions drown out your own inner voice. And most important, have the courage to follow your heart and intuition.

Steve Jobs

JULY 26

And I said to my body, softly, 'I want to be your friend.' it took a long breath and replied, "I have been waiting my whole life for this.'

Nayyirah Waheed

JULY 27

Success is finding satisfaction in giving a little more than you take.

Christopher Reeve

JULY 28

You don't have to be a genius or a visionary or even a college graduate to be successful. You just need a framework and a dream.

Michael Dell

JULY 29

Strive not to be a success, but rather to be of value.

Albert Einstein

JULY 30

The journey of a thousand miles
begins with one step.

Lao Tzu

JULY 31

There are those who look at things the way they are, and ask why... I dream of things that never were, and ask why not?

Robert Kennedy

AUGUST 1

A man must be big enough to admit his mistakes, smart enough to profit from them, and strong enough to correct them.

John C. Maxwell

AUGUST 2

Discipline is the bridge between goals and accomplishment.

Jim Rohn

AUGUST 3

Success consists of going from failure to failure without loss of enthusiasm.

Winston Churchill

AUGUST 4

The only true wisdom is in knowing
you know nothing.

Socrates

<u>AUGUST 5</u>

Do not go where the path may lead, go instead where there is no path and leave a trail.

Ralph Waldo Emerson

AUGUST 6

It's not what you look at that matters,
it's what you see.

Henry David Thoreau

AUGUST 7

The end is not the reward; the path you take, the emotions that course through you as you grasp life – that is the reward.

Jamie Magee

AUGUST 8

Your attitude, not your aptitude, will determine your altitude.

Zig Ziglar

AUGUST 9

Everything comes to us that belongs to us if we create the capacity to receive it.

Rabindranath Tagore

AUGUST 10

Be as you wish to seem.

Socrates

AUGUST 11

The greater danger for most of us lies not in setting our aim too high and falling short; but in setting our aim too low, and achieving our mark.

Michelangelo

AUGUST 12

Think twice before you speak, because your words and influence will plant the seed of either success or failure in the mind of another.

Napoleon Hill

AUGUST 13

Experience is not what happens to you; it's what you do with what happens to you.

Aldous Huxley

AUGUST 14

It is a common experience that a
problem difficult at night is resolved in
the morning after the committee of sleep
has worked on it.

John Steinbeck

AUGUST 15

Always be a first-rate version of yourself, instead of a second-rate version of somebody else.

Judy Garland

AUGUST 16

No matter what people tell you, words
and ideas can change the world.

Robin Williams

<u>AUGUST 17</u>

Life shrinks or expands in proportion
to one's courage.

Anais Nin

AUGUST 18

I have just three things to teach:
simplicity, patience, compassion. These
three are your greatest treasures.

Lao Tzu

AUGUST 19

Always seek out the seed of triumph in
every adversity.

Og Mandino

AUGUST 20

You've got to go out on a limb
sometimes because that's where the fruit
is.

Will Rogers

AUGUST 21

Everything that irritates us about others can lead us to an understanding of ourselves.

Carl Jung

AUGUST 22

Whatever you do in life, surround yourself with smart people who'll argue with you.

John Wooden

AUGUST 23

The best way to destroy an enemy is to make him a friend.

Abraham Lincoln

AUGUST 24

The art of being wise is the art of
knowing what to overlook.

William James

AUGUST 25

I'd rather regret the things I've done than regret the things I haven't done.

Lucille Ball

AUGUST 26

Never tell people how to do things. Tell them what to do and they will surprise you with their ingenuity.

George S. Patton

AUGUST 27

Imagination is more important than knowledge.

Albert Einstein

AUGUST 28

The thing that lies at the foundation of positive change, the way I see it, is service to a fellow human being.

Lech Walesa

AUGUST 29

When you are thwarted, it is your own attitude that is out of order.

Meister Eckhart

AUGUST 30

Everyone thinks of changing the world,
but no one thinks of changing himself.

Leo Tolstoy

AUGUST 31

How many cares one loses when one decides not to be something but to be someone.

Coco Chanel

SEPTEMBER 1

Use what talents you possess; the woods would be very silent if no birds sang there except those that sang best.

Henry Van Dyke

SEPTEMBER 2

Reality is merely an illusion, albeit a very persistent one.

Albert Einstein

SEPTEMBER 3

Set your course by the stars, not by the
lights of every passing ship.

Omar N. Bradley

SEPTEMBER 4

To forgive is to set a prisoner free and discover that the prisoner was you.

Lewis B. Smedes

SEPTEMBER 5

Change can be scary, but you know what's scarier? Allowing fear to stop you from growing, evolving and progressing.

Mandy Hale

SEPTEMBER 6

You've done it before and you can do it now. See the positive possibilities. Redirect the substantial energy of your frustration and turn it into positive, effective, unstoppable determination.

Ralph Marston

SEPTEMBER 7

What would life be if we had no courage
to attempt anything?

Vincent Van Gogh

SEPTEMBER 8

You are the sum total of everything you've ever seen, heard, eaten, smelled, been told, forgot - it's all there. Everything influences each of us, and because of that I try to make sure that my experiences are positive.

Maya Angelou

SEPTEMBER 9

It takes but one positive thought when given a chance to survive and thrive to overpower an entire army of negative thoughts.

Robert H. Schuller

SEPTEMBER 10

How wonderful it is that nobody need wait a single moment before starting to improve the world.

Anne Frank

SEPTEMBER 11

It's your outlook on life that counts. If you take yourself lightly and don't take yourself too seriously, pretty soon you can find the humor in our everyday lives. And sometimes it can be a lifesaver.

Betty White

SEPTEMBER 12

Perpetual optimism is a
force multiplier.

Colin Powell

SEPTEMBER 13

If you could get up the courage to begin,
you have the courage to succeed.

David Viscott

SEPTEMBER 14

My dear friend, clear your mind of can't.

Samuel Johnson

SEPTEMBER 15

People deal too much with the negative,
with what is wrong. Why not try and
see positive things, to just touch those
things and make them bloom?

Nhat Hanh

SEPTEMBER 16

There is only one thing for us to do, and that is to do our level best right where we are every day of our lives; To use our best judgment, and then to trust the rest to that Power which holds the forces of the universe in his hands.

Orison Swett Marden

SEPTEMBER 17

Once you say you're going to settle for second, that's what happens to you in life.

John F. Kennedy

SEPTEMBER 18

When someone does something good,
applaud! You will make two people
happy.

Samuel Goldwyn

SEPTEMBER 19

Like success, failure is many things to many people. With Positive Mental Attitude, failure is a learning experience, a rung on the ladder, a plateau at which to get your thoughts in order and prepare to try again.

W. Clement Stone

SEPTEMBER 20

Instead of hating, I have chosen to forgive and spend all of my positive energy on changing the world.

Camryn Manheim

SEPTEMBER 21

It is not how much we have, but how much we enjoy, that makes happiness.

Charles Spurgeon

SEPTEMBER 22

Too often we underestimate the power of a touch, a smile, a kind word, a listening ear, an honest compliment, or the smallest act of caring, all of which have the potential to turn a life around.

Leo Buscaglia

SEPTEMBER 23

What sunshine is to flowers, smiles are to humanity. These are but trifles, to be sure; but scattered along life's pathway, the good they do is inconceivable.

Joseph Addison

SEPTEMBER 24

A man can fail many times, but he isn't a
failure until he begins to blame
somebody else.

John Burroughs

SEPTEMBER 25

Ability is what you're capable of doing.
Motivation determines what you do.
Attitude determines how well you do it.

Lou Holtz

SEPTEMBER 26

If there is no struggle, there is no progress.

Frederick Douglass

SEPTEMBER 27

Never believe that a few caring people
can't change the world. For, indeed,
that's all who ever have.

Margaret Mead

SEPTEMBER 28

It may be hard for an egg to turn into a bird: it would be a jolly sight harder for it to learn to fly while remaining an egg. We are like eggs at present. And you cannot go on indefinitely being just an ordinary, decent egg. We must be hatched or go bad.

C. S. Lewis

SEPTEMBER 29

God grant me the serenity to accept the
things I cannot change, the courage to
change the things I can, and the wisdom
to know the difference.

Reinhold Niebuhr

SEPTEMBER 30

Things do not change; we change.

Henry David Thoreau

OCTOBER 1

Face the facts of being what you are, for
that is what changes what you are.

Soren Kierkegaard

OCTOBER 2

Many of life's failures are people who did not realize how close they were to success when they gave up.

Thomas A. Edison

OCTOBER 3

All changes, even the most longed for, have their melancholy; for what we leave behind us is a part of ourselves; we must die to one life before we can enter another.

Anatole France

OCTOBER 4

Smile, it's free therapy.

Douglas Horton

OCTOBER 5

What we think determines what
happens to us, so if we want to change
our lives, we need to stretch our minds.

Wayne Dyer

OCTOBER 6

Failed plans should not be interpreted as a failed vision. Visions don't change, they are only refined. Plans rarely stay the same, and are scrapped or adjusted as needed. Be stubborn about the vision, but flexible with your plan.

John C. Maxwell

OCTOBER 7

Find joy in everything you choose to do. Every job, relationship, home... it's your responsibility to love it, or change it.

Chuck Palahniuk

OCTOBER 8

Life is about not knowing, having to change, taking the moment and making the best of it, without knowing what's going to happen next.

Gilda Radner

OCTOBER 9

I'm convinced of this: Good done anywhere is good done everywhere. For a change, start by speaking to people rather than walking by them like they're stones that don't matter. As long as you're breathing, it's never too late to do some good.

Maya Angelou

OCTOBER 10

Gratitude can transform common days into thanksgivings, turn routine jobs into joy, and change ordinary opportunities into blessings.

William Arthur Ward

OCTOBER 11

The fact that I can plant a seed and it becomes a flower, share a bit of knowledge and it becomes another's, smile at someone and receive a smile in return, are to me continual spiritual exercises.

Leo Buscaglia

OCTOBER 12

When you blame others, you give up your power to change.

Robert Anthony

OCTOBER 13

Some people don't like change, but you need to embrace change if the alternative is disaster.

Elon Musk

OCTOBER 14

The time you feel lonely is the time you most need to be by yourself.

Douglas Coupland

OCTOBER 15

Isn't it amazing that we are all made in God's image, and yet there is so much diversity among his people?

Desmond Tutu

OCTOBER 16

But I am not going to live forever. And the more I know it, the more amazed I am by being here at all.

William Hurt

OCTOBER 17

You're only as young as the last time
you changed your mind.

Timothy Leary

OCTOBER 18

When it's over, I want to say: all my life
I was a bride married to amazement. I
was the bridegroom, taking the world
into my arms.

Mary Oliver

OCTOBER 19

Things alter for the worse spontaneously, if they be not altered for the better designedly.

Francis Bacon

OCTOBER 20

We cannot change anything until we accept it. Condemnation does not liberate, it oppresses.

Carl Jung

OCTOBER 21

Every day we have plenty of opportunities to get angry, stressed or offended. But what you're doing when you indulge these negative emotions is giving something outside yourself power over your happiness. You can choose to not let little things upset you.

Joel Osteen

OCTOBER 22

It is impossible for you to be angry and laugh at the same time. Anger and laughter are mutually exclusive and you have the power to choose either.

Wayne Dyer

OCTOBER 23

Serve the dinner backward, do anything - but for goodness sake, do something weird.

Elsa Maxwell

OCTOBER 24

I never learned from a man who agreed
with me.

Robert A. Heinlein

OCTOBER 25

Nothing can stop the man with the right mental attitude from achieving his goal; nothing on earth can help the man with the wrong mental attitude.

Thomas Jefferson

OCTOBER 26

The greatest day in your life and mine is when we take total responsibility for our attitudes. That's the day we truly grow up.

John C. Maxwell

OCTOBER 27

If the facts don't fit the theory,
change the facts.

Albert Einstein

OCTOBER 28

My general attitude to life is to enjoy every minute of every day. I never do anything with a feeling of, 'Oh God, I've got to do this today.'

Richard Branson

OCTOBER 29

What we achieve inwardly will change
outer reality.

Plutarch

OCTOBER 30

Having a positive mental attitude is asking how something can be done rather than saying it can't be done.

Bo Bennett

OCTOBER 31

If life were predictable it would cease to be life, and be without flavor.

Eleanor Roosevelt

NOVEMBER 1

The only disability in life is a bad attitude.

Scott Hamilton

NOVEMBER 2

The curious paradox is that when I accept myself just as I am, then I can change.

Carl Rogers

NOVEMBER 3

If you are depressed, you are living in the past. If you are anxious, living in the future. If you are at peace you are living in the moment.

Lao Tzu

NOVEMBER 4

Change will never happen when people lack the ability and courage to see themselves for who they are.

Bryant H. McGill

NOVEMBER 5

I learned that courage was not the absence of fear, but the triumph over it. The brave man is not he who does not feel afraid, but he who conquers that fear.

Nelson Mandela

NOVEMBER 6

Anger is an acid that can do more harm to the vessel in which it is stored than to anything on which it is poured.

Mark Twain

NOVEMBER 7

I cannot say whether things will get better if we change; what I can say is they must change if they are to get better.

Georg C. Lichtenberg

NOVEMBER 8

I can accept failure, everyone fails at something. But I can't accept not trying.

Michael Jordan

NOVEMBER 9

Human resources are like natural resources; they're often buried deep. You have to go looking for them, they're not just lying around on the surface. You have to create the circumstances where they show themselves.

Ken Robinson

NOVEMBER 10

The greatest test of courage on earth is
to bear defeat without losing heart.

Robert Green Ingersoll

NOVEMBER 11

'Crazy-busy' is a great armor, it's a great way for numbing. What a lot of us do is that we stay so busy, and so out in front of our life, that the truth of how we're feeling and what we really need can't catch up with us.

Brene Brown

NOVEMBER 12

If you are going to achieve excellence in big things, you develop the habit in little matters. Excellence is not an exception, it is a prevailing attitude.

Colin Powell

NOVEMBER 13

Negative emotions like loneliness, envy, and guilt have an important role to play in a happy life; they're big, flashing signs that something needs to change.

Gretchen Rubin

NOVEMBER 14

You gain strength, courage, and confidence by every experience in which you really stop to look fear in the face. You are able to say to yourself, 'I lived through this horror. I can take the next thing that comes along.'

Eleanor Roosevelt

<u>NOVEMBER 15</u>

Either you decide to stay in the shallow end of the pool or you go out in the ocean.

Christopher Reeve

NOVEMBER 16

I know of no higher fortitude than
stubbornness in the face of
overwhelming odds.

Louis Nizer

NOVEMBER 17

A positive attitude causes a chain reaction of positive thoughts, events and outcomes. It is a catalyst and it sparks extraordinary results.

Wade Boggs

NOVEMBER 18

Every great dream begins with a dreamer. Always remember, you have within you the strength, the patience, and the passion to reach for the stars to change the world.

Harriet Tubman

NOVEMBER 19

Life is the most difficult exam. Many people fail because they try to copy others, not realizing that everyone has a different question paper.

Unknown

NOVEMBER 20

I learned a long time ago the wisest thing I can do is be on my own side, be an advocate for myself and others like me.

Maya Angelou

<u>NOVEMBER 21</u>

Life is the art of drawing without
an eraser.

John W. Gardner

NOVEMBER 22

When written in Chinese, the word 'crisis' is composed of two characters. One represents danger and the other represents opportunity.

John F. Kennedy

NOVEMBER 23

A mind that is stretched by a new experience can never go back to its old dimensions.

Oliver Wendell Holmes, Jr.

NOVEMBER 24

We are not human beings having a spiritual experience. We are spiritual beings having a human experience.

Pierre Teilhard de Chardin

NOVEMBER 25

The soul should always stand ajar,
ready to welcome the ecstatic
experience.

Emily Dickinson

<u>NOVEMBER 26</u>

I have not failed. I've just found 10,000 ways that won't work.

Thomas A. Edison

<u>NOVEMBER 27</u>

Far better is it to dare mighty things, to win glorious triumphs, even though checkered by failure... than to rank with those poor spirits who neither enjoy nor suffer much, because they live in a gray twilight that knows not victory nor defeat.

Theodore Roosevelt

NOVEMBER 28

Age wrinkles the body. Quitting
wrinkles the soul.

Douglas MacArthur

NOVEMBER 29

Mistakes are the portals of discovery.

James Joyce

NOVEMBER 30

Often the difference between a successful person and a failure is not one has better abilities or ideas, but the courage that one has to bet on one's ideas, to take a calculated risk - and to act.

Andre Malraux

DECEMBER 1

Creativity requires the courage to let go of certainties.

Erich Fromm

DECEMBER 2

Any fact facing us is not as important as our attitude toward it, for that determines our success or failure. The way you think about a fact may defeat you before you ever do anything about it. You are overcome by the fact because you think you are.

Norman Vincent Peale

DECEMBER 3

Faith is taking the first step even when you don't see the whole staircase.

Martin Luther King, Jr.

DECEMBER 4

The greatest glory in living lies not in never falling, but in rising every time we fall.

Ralph Waldo Emerson

DECEMBER 5

When you focus on being a blessing,
God makes sure that you are always
blessed in abundance.

Joel Osteen

DECEMBER 6

Take the attitude of a student, never be too big to ask questions, never know too much to learn something new.

Og Mandino

DECEMBER 7

To one who has faith, no explanation is necessary. To one without faith, no explanation is possible.

Thomas Aquinas

DECEMBER 8

There is nothing that wastes the body like worry, and one who has any faith in God should be ashamed to worry about anything whatsoever.

Mahatma Gandhi

DECEMBER 9

Failure is unimportant. It takes courage
to make a fool of yourself.

Charlie Chaplin

DECEMBER 10

Faith in oneself is the best and
safest course.

Michelangelo

DECEMBER 11

We must develop and maintain the capacity to forgive. He who is devoid of the power to forgive is devoid of the power to love. There is some good in the worst of us and some evil in the best of us. When we discover this, we are less prone to hate our enemies.

Martin Luther King, Jr.

DECEMBER 12

Your problem is how you are going to spend this one odd and precious life you have been issued. Whether you're going to spend it trying to look good and creating the illusion that you have power over people and circumstances, or whether you are going to taste it, enjoy it and find out the truth about who you are.

Anne Lammott

DECEMBER 13

To keep the body in good health is a duty... otherwise we shall not be able to keep our mind strong and clear.

Buddha

DECEMBER 14

A healthy attitude is contagious but don't wait to catch it from others. Be a carrier.

Tom Stoppard

DECEMBER 15

Let your hopes, not your hurts, shape your future.

Robert H. Schuller

DECEMBER 16

I find hope in the darkest of days, and focus in the brightest. I do not judge the universe.

Dalai Lama

DECEMBER 17

You can make positive deposits in your own economy every day by reading and listening to powerful, positive, life-changing content and by associating with encouraging and hope-building people.

Zig Ziglar

DECEMBER 18

Laughter is an instant vacation.

Milton Berle

DECEMBER 19

I am not afraid of storms for I am
learning how to sail my ship.

Louisa May Alcott

DECEMBER 20

I am always doing that which I cannot do, in order that I may learn how to do it.

Pablo Picasso

DECEMBER 21

Life is a series of experiences, each one of which makes us bigger, even though sometimes it is hard to realize this. For the world was built to develop character, and we must learn that the setbacks and grieves which we endure help us in our marching onward.

Henry Ford

DECEMBER 22

Learn to get in touch with the silence within yourself, and know that everything in life has purpose. There are no mistakes, no coincidences, all events are blessings given to us to learn from.

Elisabeth Kubler-Ross

DECEMBER 23

Your mind will answer most questions if you learn to relax and wait for the answer.

William S. Burroughs

DECEMBER 24

Imagination was given to man to compensate him for what he is not; a sense of humor to console him for what he is.

Francis Bacon

DECEMBER 25

If you bring forth what is within you,
what you bring forth will save you. If
you do not bring forth what is within
you, what you do not bring forth will
destroy you.

Jesus Christ

DECEMBER 26

Learn to enjoy every minute of your life. Be happy now. Don't wait for something outside of yourself to make you happy in the future. Think how really precious is the time you have to spend, whether it's at work or with your family. Every minute should be enjoyed and savored.

Earl Nightingale

DECEMBER 27

The secret of success is learning how to use pain and pleasure instead of having pain and pleasure use you. If you do that, you're in control of your life. If you don't, life controls you.

Tony Robbins

DECEMBER 28

Creativity itself doesn't care at all about results - the only thing it craves is the process. Learn to love the process and let whatever happens next happen, without fussing too much about it. Work like a monk, or a mule, or some other representative metaphor for diligence. Love the work. Destiny will do what it wants with you, regardless.

Elizabeth Gilbert

DECEMBER 29

We are what we repeatedly do.
Excellence, then, is not an act, but a
habit.

Aristotle

DECEMBER 30

You can hope for a miracle in your life, or you can realize that your life is the miracle.

Robert Brault

<u>DECEMBER 31</u>

Life is a great big canvas, and you
should throw all the paint on it you can.

Danny Kaye

ABOUT THE AUTHOR

Erin Pizzo is a Transformational Coach, change catalyst, cancer thriver, and blogger. Erin lives in Kingston, Massachusetts with her husband, Mike and children, Aidan and Kyra. She hopes to inspire people to see the opportunities in their challenges, to start living the life of their dreams and to recognize how much power they truly possess.

For more inspiration:

Facebook
https://www.facebook.com/ErinPizzo

Twitter @ErinFPizzo

Website www.ErinPizzo.com.